THE YOUNG CYCLIST'S COMPANION

CONTENTS

38   Cycling Technique

56   Stepping It Up a Gear

I don't believe in Peter Pan, Frankenstein or Superman; all I wanna do is bicycle, bicycle, bicycle…

—

Bicycle Race, Queen, 1978

INTRODUCTION

Allow me to be a boring old fart for a moment and tell you about my first bike. It was a second-hand single speed with a back-brake and chopper style handlebars. I spray painted it gold. It was not the most elegant of bikes, but it was mine and I loved it. I grew up in the depths of rural Australia, and having a bike gave me a freedom I had never experienced before – to meet with my mates on our terms. No adults allowed, as we tore down vertiginous tracks, built jumps and competed on who could do the longest skids. Life had been so dull before I was mobile! Gradually, as I hit teenage years, I got more serious about cycling, joining clubs and racing in a more disciplined way.

This book is for any young person who has been similarly bitten by the cycling bug. From choosing the right bike to maintaining your trusty steed to improving your handling skills, it aims to raise your awareness of the way your bike works, and the way your body works alongside it. Because, in my experience, a little bit of understanding can make your ride that much more enjoyable. I've also added a chapter at the end for the hardcore enthusiasts who are thinking about joining clubs and going on group rides.

The thing about cycling, is that it's brilliant however you do it. Whether you're cycling around the park with your friends, going on longer weekend rides or joining a club, nothing beats the feeling of exhilaration and freedom that even now, many years later, I still get when I hop on my bike and head for the hills. So, in the words of Eddy Merckx, greatest cyclist of all time, 'Ride. Ride as much or as little, as long or as short as you feel. But ride'.

– Peter Drinkell

HISTORY OF THE BICYCLE

The penny farthing had one big wheel at the front and a smaller wheel at the back. The saddle was nearly four feet off the ground and it had no brakes!

The dandy horse was a great big balance bike, which you propelled by scooting along with your feet.

1818

1870

1863

The velocipede had pedals attached to the front wheel. It was nicknamed the 'boneshaker' because it was so uncomfortable.

New inventions brought the bike to where it is today:
- Caliper brakes made the bike safer to ride.
- The chain drive attached to the back wheel instead of the front wheel, making it easier to steer.
- The diamond frame and invention of the pneumatic tyre (an inflatable tube inside a rubber casing) made for a more comfortable ride.

1885 1885–1900

The safety bicycle had two wheels the same size, making it a practical means of transport for men and women alike.

The Right Bike For You

ANATOMY
OF A
BICYCLE

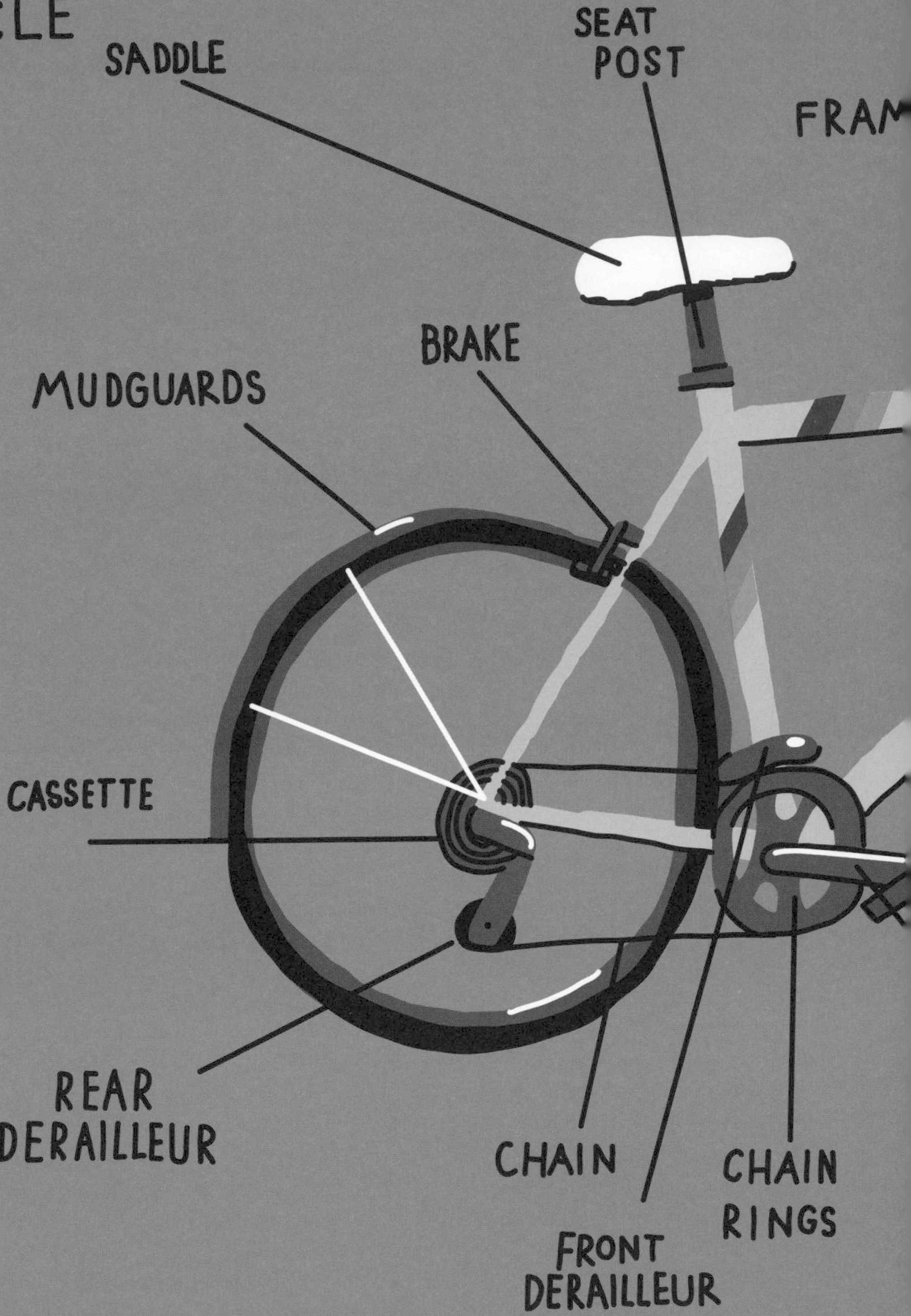

SADDLE

SEAT
POST

FRAM

BRAKE

MUDGUARDS

CASSETTE

REAR
DERAILLEUR

CHAIN

CHAIN
RINGS

FRONT
DERAILLEUR

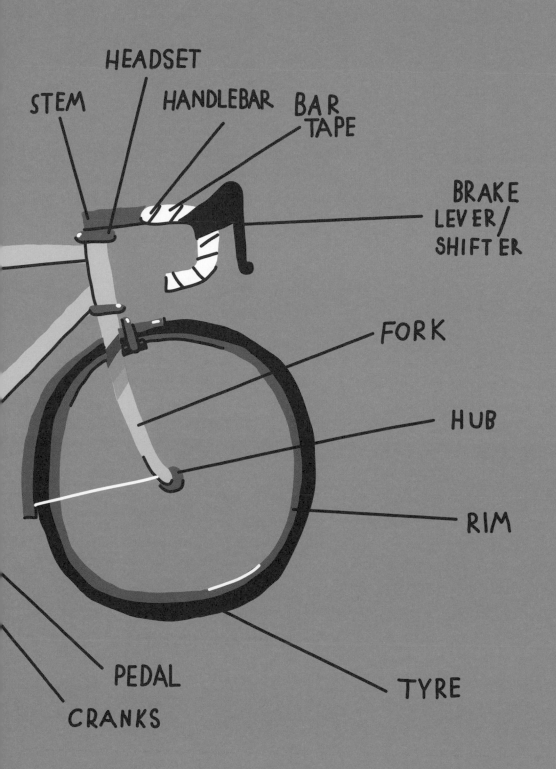

HEADSET

STEM

HANDLEBAR

BAR
TAPE

BRAKE
LEVER/
SHIFTER

FORK

HUB

RIM

PEDAL

CRANKS

TYRE

"Light. Strong. Cheap. Pick two."

—

Keith Bontrager

Choosing a Bike

There are a few things to take into account when you choose a bike. But the most important thing of all is that it has to be fun to ride. And the bikes that are the most fun to ride are the lightest, because they're also the fastest. Unfortunately, they also tend to be the most expensive.

Bikes are usually made of steel, which is heavy, or aluminium which is lighter. At the very top end, you can get a frame made of carbon fibre, which is super-light. Choose the lightest bike your money can buy and don't worry too much about fancy gears or suspension.

Ask your local bike shop for help and always take two or three different bikes for a spin before you decide. Test how they handle corners, hills and different road surfaces. Check the brakes – the brakes on a kid's bike should be very responsive.

The lightest bicycle in the world was custom built by Jason Woznick of Arizona, and weighs in at a mere 2.7 kg. The heaviest rideable bicycle weighed 1,385 kg.

Ask yourself what you will be using your bike for. Will you be cycling to school, joining a cycling club, or hurtling down rocky mountain trails? Different bicycles were developed for different purposes. Here's a thumbnail guide:

ROAD BIKE

The whippet of the cycling world, this bike has a light, stiff frame that was built for speed.

Dropped handlebars allow for a long, low, aerodynamic cycling position

All components are stripped back to make the bike as light as possible

Narrow tyres reduce friction with the road

MOUNTAIN BIKE (OR MTB)

Made for off-road cycling, mountain bikes are heavier, sturdier beasts made for durability, not speed.

Straight handlebars

Fat wheels provide traction

Disc brakes don't slip in wet weather

Suspension absorbs the shocks of riding over rocks

HYBRID BIKE

A cross between a mountain and a road bike, which makes for slightly slower but more comfortable city riding.

Riser handlebars allow you to take an upright riding position that offers a better view of the world around you

Wider tyres make for a less bumpy ride over potholes

An aluminium frame with no suspension keeps this bike light and fast

15

Bike Fit

If your bike is too big, it will be hard to control and to balance. If your bike is too small, your knees will get in the way of the handlebars, which is a) uncomfortable and b) embarrassing.

A good bike shop will measure you up for the right fit, but if you are buying your bike second-hand or online, or just want to measure yourself for fun, here's how you do it.

Firstly, measure your height by standing against a wall with no shoes on, feet hip-width apart.

Then measure your inseam as follows: still standing against a wall, feet hip-width apart, get someone to put a large book between your legs with its spine firmly against your crotch. Step away from the wall and measure from the floor to the spine of the book. This will give you your inseam measurement.

Using these measurements, work out what wheel size you need using the chart to the right. At the lowest seat position, your saddle height should be 5-7 cm higher than your inseam – so that you can touch the ground with your toes, but not put your feet flat on the floor.

This is a general size guide. The big number is the wheel size in inches. Take it with a pinch of salt – every body and every bike is different. A good bike manufacturer will list their minimum seat-post heights on their website.

Your legs power the bicycle. Your thigh-bone works like a lever. If it's longer than your shin-bone it will provide extra leverage on each stroke of the pedals.

26" Age 9-12 | Height 138-154 cm | Inseam 68-76 cm

24" Age 8-11 | Height 127-145 cm | Inseam 60-72 cm

20" Age 6-9 | Height 117-136 cm | Inseam 55-63 cm

18" Age 5-7 | Height 112-127 cm | Inseam 50-60 cm

16" Age 4-6 | Height 105-117 cm | Inseam 45-55 cm

14" Age 3-5 | Height 98-112 cm | Inseam 40-50 cm

12" Age 2-4 | Height 88-105 cm | Inseam 35-42 cm

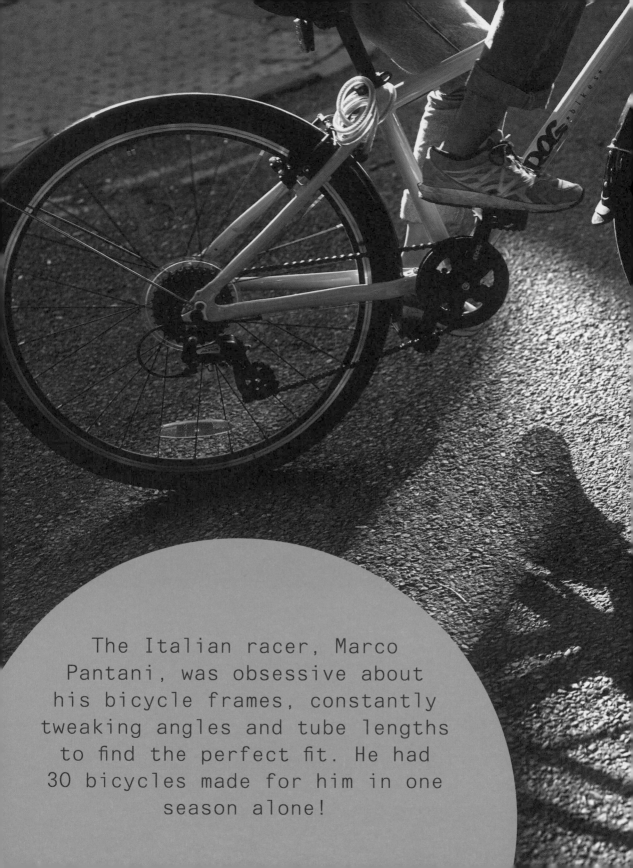

The Italian racer, Marco Pantani, was obsessive about his bicycle frames, constantly tweaking angles and tube lengths to find the perfect fit. He had 30 bicycles made for him in one season alone!

...
Other
Considerations

Tyres
Punctures are a real headache. You might want to get puncture resistant tyres. When you go for a long ride, always carry a spare inner tube or a puncture repair kit.

Saddle
If the saddle your bike came with is uncomfortable, it's worth getting a new one. Don't be fooled by looks though – sometimes most awkward looking saddles are the most comfortable!

Handlebars
When you get into more serious cycling, you'll have to choose what type of handlebars you want. There are three options:

Drop handlebars make your riding position low and aerodynamic, with your saddle higher than your hands. It's very fast, but it can be uncomfortable and is not very safe for city riding, as your eyes are down on the road, not on the world around you.

Riser handlebars and **flat handlebars** allow you to sit upright and are more common on hybrid and mountain bikes.

Moustache bars are somewhere in-between and allow you to choose between a lower or higher position.

Hi viz jacket
Depending how old/tall you are, you might be sitting quite low on the road, so always make sure cars can see you.

Helmet
Helmets are vital. Make sure you're wearing yours correctly – it should be two fingers above your eyebrows – not sitting too far back on your head.

Don't buy upgrades,
ride up grades.

—

Eddy Merckx

Bike lights are vital for visibility if you're going to be cycling in the dark or in low winter light. In some places it's illegal to cycle at night without lights.

A good lock
Invest in a strong D-lock and maybe a cable as well so that you can lock your front wheel to the back. It might well save you a lot of heartache.

2

Maintaining Your Bike

The M-Check

If you love your bike it will love you back! Every month, you should give your bike a once-over, making sure that all its components are in good condition.

The energy required to cycle at low to medium speeds is roughly the same as the energy required to walk, but four times as fast.

The M-check follows the shape of the bicycle frame, checking each of its parts in turn.

Front Wheel

Make sure your wheel nuts or quick release levers are tight. Quick release levers should be tight enough that you really have to push to close them. If you have wheel nuts, tighten them up with a spanner.

Run your hand over the spokes to check there are no loose ones. A loose spoke will need to be fixed professionally.

Spin your wheel. If it wobbles a lot from side to side, it has probably buckled and will need to be repaired or replaced at a bike shop.

Check the wheel rim. A mark along its length where the brakes rub is nothing to worry about, but if the surface bends in, it means that the wheel has worn out and may need to be replaced.

2 Tyres

Squeeze the tyre. It should be firm. If you can squeeze it in, you need to pump it up. On the rim of the tyre there will be a PSI number, which indicates the pressure that you need to pump your tyre to.

Check the surface of the tyre. If it is worn smooth it will need to be replaced. Pick out any grit that has found its way into the treads – this might cause a puncture.

I finally concluded that all failure was from a wobbling will rather than a wobbling wheel.

—

Frances E Willard

3 Brakes

Squeeze the front brake and push the bike forwards. The front wheel should hold steady, while the back wheel comes up. If the bike moves forward, you'll need to adjust the brake (see p. 31). Do the same with the back brake.

4

Handlebars

Holding the front wheel between your legs, twist the handlebars and make sure there's no side-to-side movement. Then push down on the handlebars to make sure there's no up-and-down movement. If there is, tighten it up with an Allen key.

Maintenance gets frustrating. Angering. Infuriating. That's what makes it interesting.

—

Robert M Pirsig

5

Saddle

Lift up your saddle and give it a good twist, making sure it's not moving. Also, check that your seat-post is between the markings that say 'min height, max height'. If your saddle is above the top marking, it could snap mid-ride.

6

Chain

Turn the pedals backwards and listen to the chain. Is it free running? Check the colour. Is it rusted? If so, it needs oil.

7

Back wheel

Follow the same checks as for the front wheel: spokes, braking surface, tyre surface, etc.

Cleaning

Dirty bikes are no fun to ride. The components wear down quicker and the gears will be slow to shift. Cleaning a bike can be quite relaxing, and it's a good way of getting to know all the fiddly bits of the mechanisms and how they fit together.

If you are an off-road cyclist you should clean your bike every time you ride. If you're a city cyclist, your bike will only need a scrub every three months or so – maybe a bit more frequently in winter.

1

Fill a bucket with hot water mixed with a bit of washing up liquid. Take a washing up brush and scrub the whole frame, getting into all the nooks and crannies of the chain-ring, wheels and rear cassette. Then fill up your bucket with clean hot water and sponge off the soap.

2

Use a separate sponge to clean the saddle and handlebars so you don't get grease on them.

Put a bit of washing up liquid on your hands before you work on your bike — it will make them easier to clean afterwards.

3

You'll notice that around the rear cassette, derailleur and front chainring the water is beading and the black grease is not shifting. For this you'll need a degreaser. I prefer the more environmentally friendly citrus degreasers. Use an old toothbrush to scrub all the hard-to-get bits inside the gear and chain mechanisms.

4

Once all the grease has dissolved, rinse it with hot water. If the grease still isn't coming off, use hot soapy water first, and then clean hot water. Use a rag to wipe it off - cotton is more absorbent than synthetic fabrics.

Don't use a high pressure hose to clean your bike — it can damage the bottom bracket.

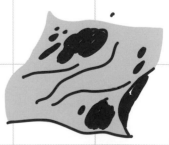

5

Dry off your bike with a clean cloth, getting into all the tight spots. Dry between the gears by running the edge of a rag between each of the gear sprockets. Dry the chain by holding a clean rag around it and spinning the pedal backwards.

Lubricating Your Bike

After you clean your bike, it's important to use lubrication to keep the components operating smoothly and prevent rust. If you're a road/city cyclist you can use a dry lube, like GT85 or WD40, which attracts less grit. Off-roaders, who are getting extra muddy, will need to use a wet lube, which is messier but sticks better to your chain and gears.

3

Lubricate the gear cables
Go to the shifters and spray at the point where the gear cables come in. Then spray the points at the front and rear of the derailleur where the cable is exposed. Then shift the gears up and down so that the oil works along the cables.

2

Lubricate the brake cables
Pull the brake levers in, and using a nozzle attachment, spray at the point where the cable comes out of the housing. Then spray the bit where the cable comes out along the top tube. Pump the brakes a few times to help the lubricant work along the cable.

1

Oil the chain
Place a rag underneath it and then dribble oil on every link of the chain while spinning the pedal backwards. Once the whole chain has been covered, take a dry rag and hold it around the chain while spinning the pedal backwards again to get rid of the excess oil.

TIP: When applying the spray lubricant, take care not to get any on your wheel rims or it can make your brakes slip.

Adjusting Your Brakes

Over time, brake pads wear down and brake cables stretch. If you have to squeeze your brake levers all the way to the handlebars, or if your bike is slipping forward when you check the brakes (see p. 25), you'll need to adjust your brakes to make for a safer, more comfortable ride.

Before you do this, check your brake pads. There is a marker on them to tell you if they are worn out. If they are, you'll need to replace them in the bike shop. If there's still some life to them, the following pages will explain how you can tighten them up yourself.

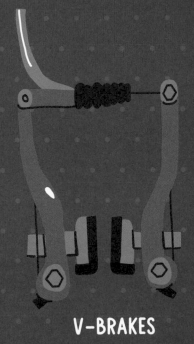

V-BRAKES

DISC BRAKES

CALIPER BRAKES

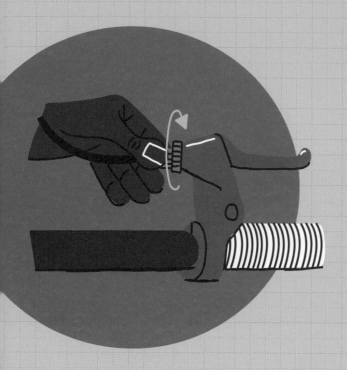

BARREL ADJUSTMENT

The easiest way to tighten your brakes is by adjusting the barrel.

On mountain bikes and hybrids with V-brakes, you can find this on the brake lever. Undo the lock-ring and then simply turn the barrel adjuster counter-clockwise. Squeeze the brakes, and when they feel tight enough, do the lock-ring back up.

On road bikes that use a caliper brake, you'll find the barrel adjuster on the brakes themselves. There's no lock-ring on these – you just turn the barrel adjuster and check to see if the caliper arms are moving in or out. Move them out until the brakes feel tight again.

ADJUSTING BRAKE CABLES ON CALIPER BRAKES

There will come a time when the brake cables are too loose to be tightened with the barrel adjuster and you'll need to shorten them. This is a trickier procedure, and you might need some help the first time you do it.

1. Start by winding the barrel adjuster all the way in, making the calipers come further apart.
2. Loosen the pinch bolt with an Allen key, holding the cable, so that the calipers don't spring apart.
3. Pull the brake blocks in tight to the rim. With the blocks in this position, pull some cable through.
4. Now tighten up the pinch bolt, securing the cable. Pump the brake lever six or seven times to take out any extra slack. It should make a big difference. If not, you'll need to repeat the process, pulling the cable in even more.

ADJUSTING THE CABLES ON V-BRAKES

1. Undo the pinch bolt on the brake arm whilst holding the loose cable in one hand, so that the brake arms don't spring apart.
2. Pull some extra cable through. When the brake pad is almost touching the rim, tighten the pinch bolt.
3. Pump the brake six or seven times to take out extra slack. If it's not tight enough, repeat the process and shorten the cable even more.

Life is like riding a bicycle. To keep your balance you must keep moving.

—

Albert Einstein

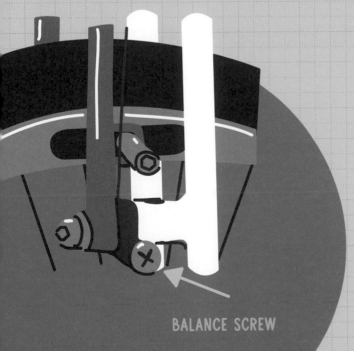

BALANCE SCREW

You may find that after you've adjusted the cable, one brake pad is sticking to the rim. If this happens, you'll need to centre the brakes. You can do this with balance screw. This is the little screw on the side of the brake arms towards the bottom. If you turn the balance screw clockwise, the pad will move toward the rim; anticlockwise will move the pad away. Adjust the pad and check whether the wheel spins freely.

33

The 1913 Tour de France rules forbade any outside assistance. When the race leader's front fork broke, he trekked 10 km to a forge where he repaired it himself. He received a 10 minute penalty, because a child worked the bellows.

How to Mend a Puncture

Mending a puncture is a fiddly business, but just imagine you're on a road trip out in the middle of nowhere and you get a flat – it could just save your bacon. So spend some time learning to do this in the comfort of your own home.

You will need:

- A spare inner tube or a puncture repair kit
- Two or three tyre levers
- A bicycle pump

1 **Find what caused the puncture** and get it the heck away from your tyre. If you can, mark the point at which the offending object entered with a bit of chalk.

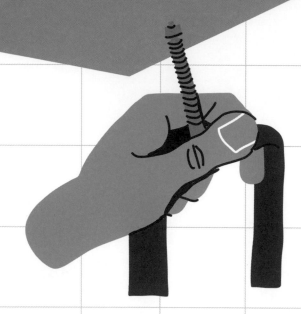

2 **Remove the wheel**
Using the wheel nut or the quick release levers, take the wheel off. You might need to let some air out to get it past the brake pads. Once you've got it off, let out any remaining air.

3 **Remove the inner tube**
Starting opposite the tyre valve, insert a tyre lever under the edge of the tyre and push it up over the rim. Hook the other end of the lever onto a spoke. Insert a second lever a couple inches further along the rim. You should be able to run the second lever all around the rim to lift the edge of the tyre off the wheel. If not, put in a third tyre lever. Once the tyre is off, push the valve through the rim and carefully pull out the inner tube.

4 **Find the hole**
If the inner tube is visibly damaged, it will need to be replaced. Otherwise, you'll need to find the hole and mend it. To do this, inflate the inner tube and run it round close to your upper lip to feel any air escaping. If you still can't find the hole, inflate the tube and put it in a sink of water. The bubbles will tell you where it is. Dry the tube and mark the hole.

Mend the puncture

Using your repair kit, roughen the area around the hole with sandpaper. Then spread glue on the area and wait a couple minutes until it becomes tacky. Peel the backing paper off the repair patch and hold it firmly onto the glued area for a couple of minutes, making sure the edges are properly glued down. Put a bit of talcum powder over the patch to keep it from sticking to the tyre.

Replace the inner tube

Before you replace the inner tube, give your tyre a check to make sure there's no shard of nastiness still lurking in there. If you marked the outside with chalk, then look on the inside in that area to make sure it's gone. Then put a little bit of air in the inner tube and push the valve stem through the hole in the rim. Gently put the inner tube back in the tyre.

Replace the tyre

About half the tyre will slot easily back into the rim, but the second half will need some help. Push the valve stem halfway back through the rim hole so that the tube doesn't get pinched, then push the tyre edge into the rim with your thumbs, starting on either side of the valve and working your way outwards. You will need to use a bit of force to get the last bit of tyre over the rim. Once it's on, push the wall of the tyre away from the rim to make sure that the inner tube hasn't got trapped under the tyre. Do this all the way around the wheel.

8

Replace the wheel

Put the wheel back into the frame, and then fully inflate the tyre. Tighten the wheel nuts or quick release levers and make sure the wheel spins freely and the brake blocks are in the correct position. Done!

Cycling Technique

Road Safety

> I can handle
> bars and cycle
> paths, but I can't
> handle cars and
> psychopaths.
>
> —
>
> Anonymous

If you are cycling in the city – even if it's a short ride to school – you need to follow the rules. You are sharing the road with a load of vehicles that are a lot bigger and more powerful than you! A lot of road safety is common sense: Always obey the highway code, stop at red lights, take care at intersections, wear a helmet and hi viz clothing, keep your bike well maintained. Don't use headphones or mobiles. Don't undertake vehicles. Don't cycle on the pavement. Don't cycle too close to parked cars. Look out for opening car doors.

Here are some additional rules that will keep you safe when cycling in the city.

Keep away from the kerb
If you cycle in the gutter, you will find that cars pretty much ignore you, which can be dangerous – especially when changing lanes or turning corners. If you ride about a meter away from the kerb (or further if there are parked cars), you'll find that cars will give you more space when overtaking.

At a junction you should be right in the middle of the lane so that cars don't edge you off the road. You might get a few honks, but ignore them. You have as much right to be there as anyone else and your safety is your priority.

Be aware of blind spots especially with lorries and other large vehicles
50% of cyclist deaths are caused by trucks, and this is mostly down to the blind spots in front, behind and to the side of a lorry. Either stay back or safely overtake on the right. Never ever undertake a vehicle when it is turning.

Glance over your shoulder
both to see what's coming up behind you and to make eye contact with drivers. If they know you're an actual person, they might treat you like one!

It's a risky business being a cyclist... there a lot of people who really dislike us... We just hope people realise we are just flesh and bones on two wheels.

—

Victoria Pendleton

What to do if you are in an accident:

1

Get out of the danger zone, and if you can't, then shout out or make yourself as visible as possible.

2

If you are injured, ask someone to call an ambulance.

3

Exchange details with the driver, take a note of their vehicle details and, if you can, take pictures of the scene (ideally before the vehicle and your bike are moved).

4

You are entitled to compensation, just as a driver would, so make sure you make a report of any damages.

Cycling is such a stupid sport. Next time you are in a car travelling at 40 mph, think about jumping out — naked. That's what it's like when we crash.
—

David Millar

Hand Signals

Hand signals allow you to communicate with drivers and cyclists coming up behind you and can help you stay safe on the road.

Indicating to turn
Hold your arm out to indicate the direction you are going to turn and glance over your shoulder to make sure it's all clear before you make the turn.

Slowing or stopping
It's good practice to indicate to cyclists behind you if you are stopping or slowing – even if you are just approaching a traffic light or intersection. Hold out a hand, palm facing the rider.

Moving out of your line
If there's a pothole or other obstacle in your way, let the rider behind you know that you're going to move to the side, as they'll probably want to do the same. Indicate with your arm behind your back. Left arm means you should move to the right, and right means to the left.

1

2

3

PERCENTAGE OF
EUROPEAN CYCLE
COMMUTERS:
COPENHAGEN 49%
AMSTERDAM 35%
BERLIN 13%
PARIS 5%
LONDON 2%
ROME 0.6%

Gearing

As you step up your cycling ambitions, you'll start taking longer and harder rides, and you'll need to use your gears properly to make your cycling technique smoother and more efficient.

Your gears can help you maintain a steady cadence. Cadence is the pace of your pedalling. The steadier you pedal, the more efficiently you can cover long distances. A pro cyclist will have a cadence of 80-90 RPM, meaning that their pedals make a full rotation 80-90 times per minute. Using their gears, they will try to keep this cadence the same on the uphill as they do on the flat.

CHAIN

FRONT DERAILLEUR

CHAINRINGS

Gears are the most complicated part of your bike and it takes a bit of time to figure out how they work and how to make the most of them. In very simple terms you use a low gear to make it easier to pedal and a high gear to go faster.

In more complex terms it works like this: The front gears are referred to as chainrings. Most bikes have either two or three chainrings. The smallest chainring is closest to the frame and is the easiest to pedal on. As you move away from the bike, the chainrings get bigger. The larger the chainring, the harder it is to pedal and the faster you go.

The gears on the rear wheel are called the cassette. It is made of smaller rings called 'cogs'. Most bikes have between eight and 11 cogs. The largest cogs are closest to the frame, getting smaller as you move out. The larger the cog, the easier it is to pedal, the smaller the cog the faster you go.

As you get used to using your gears, you'll get more out of them. These are some basic gearing rules:

1

Avoid cross-chaining – this is when you have a little-little or big-big combination (littlest/biggest chairing to littlest/biggest cog). This will cause your chain to rub and wear your components down.

2

Anticipate gear changes. If you shift your gears a fraction before you have to, you can keep your pedalling steady without slowing down as you crank through the gear change.

3

Keep pedalling, even when you're on the downhill! This will help you maintain balance and control.

Bike companies like to show off how many 'speeds' a bike has, but if you have two chainrings and nine cogs, you don't really have 18 gears, because a lot of them overlap. Pro cyclists only refer to the number of cogs — so they would refer to that bike as nine speed.

It's a little like wrestling a gorilla. You don't stop when you're tired, you stop when the gorilla is tired.

Fausto Coppi

Braking

Your bike has two brakes – one at the front and one at the back. Your front brake is the more effective one – if you grab it hard, the bike can stop very suddenly, skidding or sending you over the handlebars. Your back brake is better at slowing you down gradually. When braking, it's important to use both your brakes.

If you need to stop suddenly, squeeze harder on your front brake, locking your arms out in front to brace yourself against the sudden stop. However, where possible, it's better to 'feather' your brakes – pump them gently and repeatedly – so that the stop is gradual. This is especially important if there are cyclists coming up behind you.

Braking in wet conditions is a bit trickier, as the brakes are less effective and skids are more likely. In these conditions, make more use of your back brake to slow you down. If you're on a steep downhill or need to make a sudden stop, it's best to brake hard, release, then brake hard again. This reduces the chance of skidding.

Descending

Racing downhill is exhilarating and terrifying in equal measure. As you become more confident you can take those straight drops at speed.

Keep your body low to the bike to reduce wind resistance, but always look ahead – obstacles come up on you quickly when you're descending!

Sit slightly up off the saddle – this will give you a bit of natural suspension.

Keep a relaxed grip on the bars. Tensing up will make your handling less efficient.

Ride it like you
stole it.
—

Anonymous

48

Cornering

1

Only take wide corners at speed. In wet conditions and on very tight corners, take it very slow. Make sure you slow down before you hit the corner, not when you're already in it.

•••

When you're going down a long mountain road, you'll find that the bends in the road can really slow you down. If you want to maximise your speed on the descent, you need to flow smoothly in and out of the corners. Some tips:

2

Keep your body and the bike in line. Lean into the corner with your body and the bike, shifting your weight slightly back in the saddle.

3

Always look beyond the corner, so you can predict what's coming next.

4

Enter and exit the corner as wide as you can, so you're straightening it out as much as possible.

5

Keep your inside leg up and your outside leg straight to prevent your pedal touching the ground and potentially flipping you off the bike.

49

In Victorian times,
cycle races were banned
in Britain, as cyclists
were considered too
reckless. As a result,
people raced in secret
time trials, setting off
at one minute intervals
and dressed in black to
look less conspicuous.
In 1882, even a
gentleman of a 'most
respectable address'
was fined 30 shillings
for riding through
London at a 'furious'
10 miles per hour.

Wheelie

It is actually illegal to do a wheelie on a road in the UK and for good reason. It's lethally dangerous and actually pretty pointless for any purpose other than showing off. So, having warned you of the dangers, here's how to do it:

The wheelie is a surprisingly difficult trick. It requires coordination, strength and balance. To begin with, practice on a slight uphill slope. It's easier and safer. Also, practice hopping off the back halfway through. It might well save you a concussion or two.

You ride the wheelie sitting down. Put your seat in its lowest position. Keeping a low centre of gravity will help your balance.

With your bike in a low gear, and your pedals at a 10:00 position, crouch your upper body over the handlebars.

Pedal down and pull up on the handlebars simultaneously, then immediately lean back. Don't stop pedalling, but don't pedal too fast or your speed will become uncontrollable.

Approximately 105 million bicycles are made every year — that's double the number of cars produced. There are estimated to be around a billion bicycles in existence, with China accounting for about half of them.

4

Keep your arms outstretched and your bum at the back edge of the saddle.

5

Feather your back brake continuously to control your speed and your vertical balance.

6

Once you're up in the air, control your sideways balance by turning the handlebars in the opposite direction or by sticking out a knee. The balance constantly needs to be adjusted as you ride.

7

To come out of the move, make sure your handlebars are straight and then let the front wheel drop.

Bunny Hops

Bunny hopping is when you lift both wheels off the ground simultaneously. Unlike wheelies, this is actually quite a useful trick when you're cycling in a group. It allows you to jump over obstacles and maintain a straight line, rather than swerving.

1

Place a rolled towel or similar on the ground. Cycle towards it at around 15 km/h (not too fast).

2

As you approach the towel, stop your pedals at a horizontal position. Lift your bum out of the saddle and shift your weight forward so you're in a crouched position towards the handlebars.

3

Spring upwards, pulling on the handlebars at the same time that you explode up with your legs so that both wheels come off the ground simultaneously.

Try lifting the front wheel and back wheel separately at first. Then do small bunny hops without jumping over an obstacle. When you're confident with these, then try with the towel.

4

Try to land softly with bent knees and elbows, so that your front wheel doesn't slap onto the ground.

Stepping It
Up a Gear

Group Riding

If you've really caught the cycling bug, you might be thinking about joining a cycling club. Cycling clubs are a great way of getting expert coaching, meeting fellow cycle-enthusiasts and accessing cool facilities. They are also the best way of getting to grips with group cycling. Group cycling is very different to riding solo, because it's not just about pedalling, but about how you work alongside other riders for a more efficient, enjoyable ride.

Training can be monotonous and it is hard work, but you never lose sight of why you are doing it. Every single effort of every single session counts in the months and years leading up to a big event.

—

Chris Hoy

Drafting

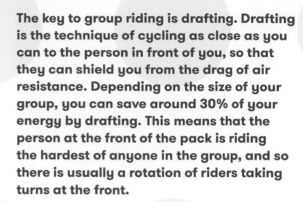

The key to group riding is drafting. Drafting is the technique of cycling as close as you can to the person in front of you, so that they can shield you from the drag of air resistance. Depending on the size of your group, you can save around 30% of your energy by drafting. This means that the person at the front of the pack is riding the hardest of anyone in the group, and so there is usually a rotation of riders taking turns at the front.

Drafting can be quite daunting to begin with, as you need to keep a perfectly steady pace with the people in front and behind you to avoid collisions.

A good way to start is by practicing with one or two other riders. Pro cyclists can safely keep an inch between their front wheel and the back wheel of the rider in front, but to begin with you should probably stay a bike length behind, bringing that down as your skill level and bike-handling improves.

Cycling is based so much on form, on aesthetics, on class — the way you carry yourself on the bike, the sort of technique you have.

—

David Millar

Drafting Rules

These are some drafting rules to bear in mind when you start group riding:

1

Practice holding a straight line and maintaining a steady cadence (see p. 44).

2

Make all your moves obvious and predictable. No sudden swerves or braking. If you do need to stray from your line, make sure you use hand signals to warn the cyclist behind (see p. 43).

3

When you get up out of the saddle, your bike can surge backwards, so increase your pace slightly to create a bit of space before getting up.

4

Keep an eye on the road ahead, so that you can smoothly change gears without slowing down.

5

Never allow your wheel to cross over with that of the person in front. If they make a sudden move sideways you'll both take a tumble.

6

Listen to the advice of more experienced riders, even if you're a strong cyclist. There is no room for a hot-head on a group ride.

7

When you start out, hang back and give yourself space to safely follow the wheel in front. A good group will accommodate any skill level. As long as you behave respectfully to your fellow riders, nobody will mind slowing down for you.

Clipless Pedals

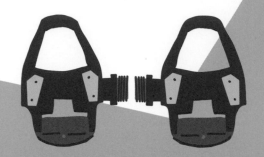

If you are considering moving into more serious road cycling, clipless pedals are essential. The name is deceptive; you actually clip into clipless pedals using special shoes with a cleat on the sole. This holds your foot in place, so that you can efficiently channel power directly into the pedals.

When you stop pedalling, you need to unclip your shoes, or you'll topple over. Clipping in and out takes a bit of getting used to, so practice on a quiet stretch of road with a grassy verge before you try this on a busy street. Once you're used to it, try to stay clipped in as long as possible, only clipping out just before you need to stop.

Other Kit

These are less essential but still useful pieces of kit for a budding road cyclist.

Cycling jerseys are made from a light, breathable material that is engineered for comfort. It should be close fitting for maximum aerodynamics. Cycling jerseys have three pockets at the back for your essentials, so you don't need to carry a cumbersome bag.

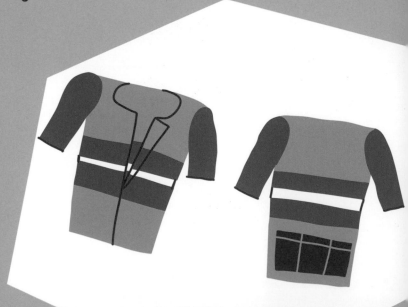

Bib shorts have padding called a chamois in the crotch, which protects you from chafing in the saddle, whilst still allowing a maximum range of movement. These are usually preferred to cycling shorts, as they cover your mid-section when you're taking your aerodynamic position.

Cycling glasses are specially designed not to shatter. They protect your eyes not just from the sun but from grit and flying debris. It looks better if you wear the arms of your glasses over the straps of your helmet – not under!

Gloves
Not everyone likes wearing cycling gloves, but they offer protection from road rash in case of a fall.

It never gets easier. You just get faster.

—

Greg LeMond

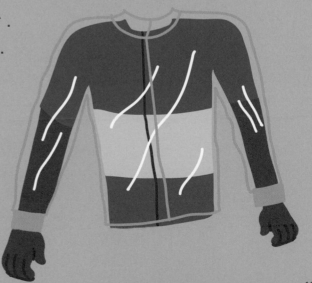

Rain cape
A very light rain cape tucked into the pocket of your cycling jersey is always advisable. Especially on long rides.

PRO CYCLING
The Tour de France

A relaxing way of improving your group cycling technique is to watch professional cycling. This is a good place to mention that cycling (like a lot of sports) is pretty sexist. Women don't compete in the Grand Tours, and in other areas of cycling, like track and cyclo-cross, women are paid less and are much less celebrated. This is gradually changing. As more girls and women join the clubs (which are all unisex), there will be more women moving into pro cycling – as well as a bigger audience for women's sports. In the meantime, we have to make do with the outdated traditions of races that were set up over 100 years ago.

The Tour de France is the world's most famous, and most challenging bicycle race. Established in 1903, it lasts for three weeks and covers 3600 km. It is made up of different stages covering stretches of flat land and treacherous mountain climbs. There is a racing element and also a time trial element. Winners of various aspects of the tour are awarded with cycling jerseys.

The yellow jersey is the big prize. It goes to the person with the lowest cumulative cycle time over the course of the whole race.

The Tour goes on day after day after day. It's the only race in the world where you have to get a haircut halfway through.

—

Chris Boardman

The polka-dot jersey is awarded to the 'king of the mountains' – the person who has won most points in the climbing stages of the race.

The green jersey goes to the person who has been awarded the most points at the various stages of the race.

The white jersey goes to a cyclist aged 25 or younger with the lowest cumulative time.

There are usually around 20 teams participating in the Tour, with nine (male) riders on each team. Most of these team riders will not be expecting to win a jersey. Their job is to help their lead rider by letting him benefit from drafting behind them, by setting a strong pace for him, by giving him their bike if his goes wrong and by chasing down major rivals. This is group riding at its most selfless!

The two other Grand Tours (as the big, three-week road races are called) are the Giro d'Italia and the Vuelta a España.

These Tours follow similar rules to those of the Tour de France.

From an average speed of 24 km/h in 1926, the average speed of the Tour de France peaked in 2005 at close to 42 km/h.

Other Types of Racing

Road racing is the most widely followed bicycle sport, but there are other types of pro cycling that you might be interested in watching or getting involved with.

Track Cycling

Track cycling happens on specially built tracks or velodromes. Using track bicycles with only one fixed gear and no brakes, cyclists will compete in either sprint or endurance races, cycling round and round the track, using the steeply banked sides to overtake their competitors. Unlike the Grand Tours, track cycling is a sport for women as well as men. The biggest event is the UCI Track Cycling World Championships, which happens every year around April.

Amanda Coker is an American ultra-cyclist and the current record holder of the World Endurance Record for distance in a calendar year. In 2017, she beat her own world record, cycling 140,000 km.

Mountain Bike Racing (MTB)

Off-road mountain-bike racing was only officially recognised in 1990, even though MTB races have happened since the sport was invented in California in the 1970s. The two main types of MTB racing are cross-country (XC), which covers around 50 km on varied terrain; and downhill (DH), which is a time trial event down a steep, rough track.

> If you try to win, you might lose, but if you don't try to win, you lose for sure!
>
> —
>
> Jens Voigt

Cyclo-Cross (CX)

Cyclo-cross is popular in Belgium and the Netherlands. Cyclists ride laps around a relatively short course (around 3 km), which includes wooded trails, grass and pavement. There are obstacles on route that require the rider to dismount, carry the bike and remount it. Cycle-cross is raced in the winter months, and originated to allow road cyclists to compete during the off-season.

Ride as much or as little,
as long or as short as
you feel. But ride.

—

Eddy Merckx

Glossary of cycling terms

Aero – short for aerodynamic this refers to kit that is designed to reduce wind resistance.

Attack – also known as a breakaway – a sudden attempt to pull ahead in a race.

Bead – the edge of the tyres that slots into the rim of the wheel.

Bibs – cycling shorts with a bib that goes over your shoulders.

Bonk – also known as 'hitting the wall', this is when you burn through your energy resources, causing cramping and dizziness. High carb snacks and plenty of water will help recovery.

Bunny hop – a technique in which you use your arms and legs to lift both wheels off the ground.

Cadence – the revolutions per minute (RPM) of your pedals. Weaker cyclists are more efficient at a lower cadence and stronger riders are more efficient at a higher cadence.

Cassette – the pyramid-shaped set of sprockets on the rear wheel.

Century – a 100-mile ride or race.

Chainrings – the circular metal discs near the pedals. Most bikes have one, two or three chainrings.

Chamois (or shammy) – the pad in the seat of cycling shorts that wicks away moisture and provides cushioning.

Chasers – racers who pull away from the pack to try and catch up with a lead rider ahead of them.

Cleat – a metal or plastic fitting on the sole of a cycling shoe that clicks into your clipless pedals.

Climb – a hill or mountain.

Clipless – a type of pedal that locks into the cleat of special cycling shoes for better power transfer when pedalling.

Crank (or crankarm) – the arm that connects the pedals to the chainrings.

Cog – a sprocket on the rear wheel's cassette.

Criterium (or crit) – a short cycling race on city streets covering 5 km or less.

Cross-chaining – when the chain is either on the big ring at the front and the big ring at the back, or on the small ring in the front and the smallest ring at the back. This can damage your chain.

Derailleur – the mechanism that moves the chain from gear to gear when you shift.

Drafting – cycling behind another rider so they block the wind for you, saving around 30% of your energy.

Drivetrain – the entire mechanical system that converts pedalling into forward movement, including pedals, cranks, derailleurs, chainrings, cassette and chain.

Downhill – a type of mountain biking and racing.

Drops – the lower, curved part of a road bicycle's handlebars.

Endo – short for 'end over end', this means to crash by going over the bike's handlebars.

Fixie (or fixed gear) – a single-speed bike that can't freewheel (your pedals keep moving even on the downhill).

Grand Tour – One of three, three-week-long European races that involve a mix of individual and team time trials, mountain climbs and sprints. They are the Tour de France, the Giro d'Italia and Vuelta a España.

Hammer – pedalling hard in the big gears, which have the greatest resistance and pack the most power.

Half wheel – when you're cycling behind someone and your front wheel creeps on their back wheel. Very dangerous!

Headset – the parts at the top and bottom of the frame's head tube, into which the handlebar stem and fork are fitted.

Jersey – zip up jerseys that wick away sweat and have pockets on the back for essentials.

Lid – helmet

Lube – a lubricant that keeps moving parts moving.

Overgear – using a gear ratio too big for the terrain or level of fitness.

Peloton – also called a bunch or a pack, this is the largest pack of riders in a road race.

PSI – pounds per square inch; the amount of air pressure in the tyre. Your ideal PSI will be marked on the rim of your tyres.

Pull – riding on the front of a paceline or peloton. To 'take a pull' means you're the person working the hardest since you're not benefiting from drafting.

Reach – the combined length of a bike's top tube and stem, which determines the rider's distance to the handlebars.

Roadie – a nickname for a dedicated road cyclist.

Road rash – the scrapes and burns you get from crashing on the road.

Sit on a wheel – to ride in someone's draft.

Slingshot – to ride up behind another cyclist with help from their draft, then use the momentum to sprint past.

Slipstream – the pocket of air behind a cyclist that breaks the wind resistance when you're drafting.

Squirrel – a nervous or unstable rider who can't be trusted to maintain a steady line.

Time trial (TT) – a race against the clock in which individual riders start at intervals, so can't benefit from drafting.

Velodrome – an oval, banked track for bicycle racing.

Wheelie – A trick in which the front wheel is lifted off the ground whilst the bike continues to move forward.

Wheelsucker – someone who drafts behind others but doesn't take a pull.

Index

The Young Cyclist's Companion

Text © Peter Drinkell
Photography © Peter Drinkell
Illustrations © Thomas Slater

Design by April

British Library Cataloguing-in-Publication Data.

A CIP record for this book is available from the British Library.
ISBN: 978-1-908714-96-1
First published 2021

Printed in China

Cicada Books Ltd
48 Burghley Road
London NW5 1UE
www.cicadabooks.co.uk